Andrea—
Happy Graduation,
and many happy years
ahead—
June 10. 1981

Barbara

Paul

SCOTT

Ann

Little Things

Edited by Louise Bachelder

Illustrated by Pat Stewart

The Peter Pauper Press
MOUNT VERNON · NEW YORK

LITTLE drops of water, little grains of sand,
Make the mighty ocean and the pleasant land.
So the little moments, humble though they be,
Make the mighty ages of Eternity.

Little deeds of kindness, little words of love,
Help to make earth happy, like the heaven
above.

Julia A. Fletcher Carney

Little Things

Half the joy of life is in little things taken on the run. Let us run if we must — even the sands do that — but let us keep our hearts young and our eyes open that nothing worth our while shall escape us. And everything is worth while if we only grasp it and its significance.

Victor Cherbuliez

The least flower, with a brimming cup, may stand
And share its dew-drop with another near.

Elizabeth Barrett Browning

One of the most difficult things to give away is kindness, for it is usually returned.

Anonymous

NEVER lose an opportunity of seeing anything that is beautiful; for beauty is God's handwriting — a wayside sacrament. Welcome it in every fair face, in every fair sky, in every fair flower, and thank God for it as a cup of blessing.

Ralph Waldo Emerson

WHAT sunshine is to flowers, smiles are to humanity. They are but trifles, to be sure; but, scattered along life's pathway, the good they do is inconceivable.

Joseph Addison

IF you confer a benefit, never remember it; if you receive one, never forget it.

Chilo

To me the meanest flower that blows can give Thoughts that do often lie too deep for tears.

William Wordsworth

CONSIDER the postage stamp: It secures success by sticking to one thing until it gets there.

Josh Billings

How often it is difficult to be wisely chari-
table — to do good without multiplying the
sources of evil. To give alms is nothing un-
less you give thought also. It is written, not
"blessed is he that feedeth the poor," but
"blessed is he that considereth the poor." A
little thought and a little kindness are often
worth more than a great deal of money.

John Ruskin

IF you can sit at set of sun
And count the deeds that you have done
    And counting find
One self-denying act, one word
That eased the heart of him that heard —
    One glance most kind,
Which fell like sunshine where he went,
Then you may count that day well spent.

Robert Browning

WHEN I see the elaborate study and ingenu-
ity displayed by women in the pursuit of
trifles, I feel no doubt of their capacity for
the most herculean undertakings.

Julia Ward Howe

FLOWERS come to finished bloom and beauty in wilderness where no eye of man ever looked. In the conduct of life, small perfections show character; for they spring from a higher fidelity than human eye-service. He that is faithful in little is faithful also in much.

Anonymous

WRITE injuries in sand, but benefits in marble.

French Proverb

I WOULD not enter on my list of friends
(Though graced with polished manners and
    fine sense
Yet wanting sensibility) the man
Who needlessly sets foot upon a worm.

William Cowper

BETTER a diamond with a flaw than a pebble without.

Confucius

BE pleasant until 10 o'clock in the morning and the rest of the day will take care of itself.

Elbert Hubbard

LIFE is made up, not of great sacrifices or duties, but of little things, in which smiles and kindness and small obligations, given habitually, are what win and preserve the heart and secure comfort.

Sir Humphrey Davy

BENEVOLENT feeling ennobles the most trifling actions.

William Makepeace Thackeray

THE best portion of a good man's life —
  His little, nameless, unremembered acts
    Of kindness and love.

William Wordsworth

THE creation of a thousand forests is in one acorn.

Ralph Waldo Emerson

BUT words are things, and a small drop of ink, falling like dew, upon a thought, produces that which makes thousands, perhaps millions, think.

Lord Byron

WE act as though comfort and luxury were the chief requirements of life, when all we need to make us really happy is something to be enthusiastic about.

Charles Kingsley

NOT a flower
But shows some touch, in freckle, streak or
   stain,
Of His unrivall'd pencil. He inspires
Their balmy odors, and imparts their hues,
And bathes their eyes with nectar, and
   includes
In grains as countless as the seaside sands
The forms with which He sprinkles all the
   earth.

William Cowper

A WORD in earnest is better than a speech.

Charles Dickens

MOST persons would succeed in small things if they were not troubled with great ambitions.

Henry Wadsworth Longfellow

LIFE is a tender thing and is easily molested. There is always something that goes amiss. Vain vexations — vain sometimes, but always vexations. The smallest and slightest impediments are the most piercing; and as little letters most tire the eyes, so do little affairs most disturb us.

Michel de Montaigne

Do not delay; the golden moments fly!

Henry Wadsworth Longfellow

THERE are strange ways of serving God;
You sweep a room or turn a sod,
And suddenly, to your surprise,
You hear the whirr of seraphim,
And find you're under God's own eyes
And building palaces for Him.

Herman Hagedorn

A HANDFUL of pine-seed will cover mountains with the green majesty of forest. I too will set my face to the wind and throw my handful of seed on high.

William Sharp

HE has achieved success who has lived well, laughed often and loved much; who has gained the respect of intelligent men and the love of little children; who has filled his niche and accomplished his task; who has left the world better than he found it, whether by an improved poppy, a perfect poem or a rescued soul; who has never lacked appreciation of earth's beauty or failed to express it; who has looked for the best in others and given the best he had; whose life was an inspiration; whose memory is a benediction.

Mrs. Arthur J. Stanley

HE gives twice who gives quickly.

Latin Proverb

INSECTS

HAVE made the lion mad ere now; a shaft
I' the heel o'erthrew the bravest of the brave.

Lord Byron

THE reason I beat the Austrians is, they did not know the value of five minutes.

Napoleon

TRIFLES discover a character more than actions of importance. In regard to the former a person is off his guard, and thinks it not material to use disguise.

William Shenstone

ALL service ranks the same with God:
If now, as formerly He trod
Paradise, His presence fills
Our earth, each only as God wills
Can work — God's puppets, best and worst,
Are we; there is no last nor first.

Say not "a small event"! Why "small"?
Costs it more pain than this, ye call
A "great event," should come to pass,
Than that? Untwine me from the mass
Of deeds which make up life, one deed
Power shall fall short in or exceed!

Robert Browning

THE weakest among us has a gift, however seemingly trivial, which is peculiar to him, and which worthily used, will be a gift to his race forever.

John Ruskin

HE that has a "spirit of detail" will do better in life than many who figured beyond him in the university. Such an one is minute and particular. He adjusts trifles; and these trifles compose most of the business and happiness of life. Great events happen seldom, and affect few; trifles happen every moment to everybody; and though one occurrence of them adds little to the happiness or misery of life, yet the sum total of their continual repetition is of the highest consequence.

Daniel Webster

IF you would have a hen lay, you must bear with her cackling.

Proverb

PRACTICE yourself, for heaven's sake, in little things; and thence proceed to greater.

Epictetus

HE that is faithful in that which is least is faithful also in much: and he that is unjust in the least is unjust also in much.

St. Luke 16:10

NOTHING is too little which relates to man's salvation, nor is there anything too little in which either to please God or to serve Satan.

Edward Bouverie Pusey

To pursue trifles is the lot of humanity; and whether we bustle in a pantomime, or strut at a coronation, or shout at a bonfire, or harangue in a senate house — whatever object we follow, it will at last conduct us to futility and disappointment. The wise bustle and laugh as they walk in the pageant, but fools bustle and are important; and this probably is all the difference between them.

Oliver Goldsmith

TIME's corrosive dewdrop eats
　The giant warrior to a crust
　Of earth in earth and rust in rust.

Francis Turner Palgrave

EARTH's crammed with Heaven
And every common bush afire with God.
But only he who sees takes off his shoes.

Elizabeth Barrett Browning

GREAT merit, or great failings, will make you respected or despised; but trifles, little attentions, mere nothings, either done or neglected, will make you either liked or disliked in the general run of the world.

Lord Chesterfield

PERFECTION is attained by slow degrees; she requires the hand of time.

Voltaire

GIVE plenty of what is given to you,
  And listen to pity's call;
Don't think the little you give is great
  And the much you get is small.

Phoebe Cary

SMALL courtesies sweeten life; the greater ennoble it.

Christian N. Bovée

HAIL the small sweet courtesies of life, for smooth do they make the road of it.

Laurence Sterne

A LITTLE house well filled, a little land well tilled, and a little wife well willed, are great riches.

Proverb

How far that little candle throws his beams! So shines a good deed in a naughty world.

William Shakespeare

I BELIEVE a leaf of grass is no less than the
    journey-work of the stars,
And the pismire is equally perfect, and a
    grain of sand, and the egg of the wren,
And the tree-toad is a chef-d'oeuvre of the
    highest. . . .
And a mouse is miracle enough to stagger
    sextillions of infidels.

Walt Whitman

THE beginnings of all things are small.

Cicero

LITTLE things console us because little things affect us.

Blaise Pascal

THERE is a beautiful Indian apologue, which says: A man once said to a lump of clay, "What art thou?" The reply was, "I am but a lump of clay, but I was placed beside a rose and I caught its fragrance."

William Morley Punshon

THE golden poppy is God's gold,
   The gold that lifts, nor weighs us down,
The gold that knows no miser's hold,
   The gold that banks not in the town,
But singing, laughing, freely spills
Its hoard far up the happy hills;
Far up, far down, at every turn —
What beggar has not gold to burn!

Joaquin Miller

DON'T make yourself a mouse or the cat will eat you.

Proverb

LITTLE minds are too much hurt by little things; great minds are quite conscious of them, and despise them.

François, Duc de la Rochefoucauld

TRIFLES make up the happiness or the misery of mortal life. The majority of men slip into their graves without having encountered on their way thither any signal catastrophe or exaltation of fortune or feeling.

Alexander Smith

A WEED is a plant whose virtues have not been discovered.

Ralph Waldo Emerson

THAT low man seeks a little thing to do,
   Sees it and does it;
This high man, with a great thing to pursue,
Dies ere he knows it.

Robert Browning

IF everyone gives one thread, the poor man will have a shirt.

Russian Proverb

A HABIT cannot be tossed out the window; it must be coaxed down the stairs a step at a time.

Mark Twain

As daylight can be seen through very small holes, so little things will illustrate a person's character.

Samuel Smiles

SMALL opportunities are often the beginning of great enterprises.

Demosthenes

I FIND letters from God dropped in the street, and every one is signed by God's name,
And I leave them where they are, for I know that wheresoe'er I go,
Others will punctually come for ever and ever.

Walt Whitman

LIFE's great opportunities often open on the road of daily duties.

Anonymous

I HAVE seldom known anyone who deserted truth in trifles, that could be trusted in matters of importance.

William Paley

I SOMETIMES think that the most plaintive ditty has brought a fuller joy and of longer duration to its composer than the conquest of Persia to the Macedonian.

Walter Savage Landor

List to that bird! His song — what poet
    pens it?
  Brigand of birds, he's stolen every note!
Prince though of thieves — hark! how the
    rascal spends it!
  Pours the whole forest from one tiny
    throat.

Ednah Proctor (Clarke) Hayes

EVERY why hath a wherefore.

William Shakespeare

THERE is nothing insignificant — nothing.

Samuel Taylor Coleridge

I OWE all my success in life to having been always a quarter of an hour beforehand.

Lord Nelson

DESPISE not small things, either for evil or good, for a look may work thy ruin, or a word create thy wealth. — A spark is a little thing, yet it may kindle the world.

Martin Farquhar Tupper

ILL habits gather by unseen degrees —
As brooks make rivers, rivers run to seas.

John Dryden

OH, many a shaft at random sent
Finds mark the archer little meant!
And many a word at random spoken
May soothe, or wound, a heart that's broken.

Sir Walter Scott

HE who would eat the kernel must crack the shell.

Plautus

THERE are no trifles in the moral universe of God. Speak but one true word today, and it shall go ringing on through the ages.

William Morley Punshon

WHOEVER shall review his life will find that the whole tenor of his conduct has been determined by some accident of no apparent moment.

Samuel Johnson

YOU'D scarce expect one of my age
To speak in public on the stage;
And if I chance to fall below
Demosthenes or Cicero,
Don't view me with a critic's eye,
But pass my imperfections by.
Large streams from little fountains flow,
Tall oaks from little acorns grow.
These thoughts inspire my youthful mind
To be the greatest of mankind;
Great, not like Cæsar, stained with blood,
But only great as I am good.
  [*Lines written for the school declamation
  of a seven-year-old boy in 1791*]

David Everett

GIVE what you have. To some one, it may be better than you dare to think.

Henry Wadsworth Longfellow

It matters not how small the beginning may seem to be: what is once well done is done forever.

Henry David Thoreau

A HANDFUL of common sense is worth a bushel of learning.

Proverb

It is not growing like a tree
  In bulk, doth make man better be;
Or standing long an oak tree, three hundred
    year,
To fall a log at last, dry, bald, and sear:
    A lily of a day
    Is fairer far in May,
  Although it fall and die that night—
  It was the plant and flower of Light.
In small proportions we just beauties see,
And in short measures life may perfect be.

Ben Jonson

THINK in the morning. Act in the noon. Eat in the evening. Sleep in the night.

William Blake

To us also, through every star, through every blade of grass, is not a God made visible if we will open our mind and eyes?

Thomas Carlyle

HEREBY I learned have, not to despise,
What ever thing seems small in common eyes.

Edmund Spenser

SOME have too much, yet still do crave;
   I little have, and seek no more:
They are but poor, though much they have,
   And I am rich with little store:
They poor, I rich; they beg, I give;
They lack, I leave; they pine, I live.

Edward Dyer

BETTER be proficient in one art than a smatterer in a hundred.

Japanese Proverb

MOST of the critical things in life, which become the starting points of human destiny, are little things.

Roswell Smith

IF I had but two loaves of bread, I would sell one and buy hyacinths, for they would feed my soul.

The Koran

So don't despise the little things
    Which happen daily round us,
For some of them may chance take wings
    To startle and astound us.
Trace back the greatest deed — it springs
From trifles which no poet sings.

Charles Graham Halpine

GOOD thoughts, even if they are forgotten, do not perish.

Publilius Syrus

THE most wasted of days is that in which one has not laughed.

Sebastian R. N. Chamfort

A GRAIN of sand leads to the fall of a mountain when the moment has come for the mountain to fall.

Ernest Renan

THE mind of the greatest man on earth is not so independent of circumstances as not to feel inconvenienced by the merest buzzing noise about him; it does not need the report of a cannon to disturb his thoughts. The creaking of a vane or a pulley is quite enough. Do not wonder that he reasons ill just now; a fly is buzzing by his ear; it is quite enough to unfit him for giving good counsel.

Blaise Pascal

OH, the little more, and how much it is!
And the little less, and what world away!

Robert Browning

THE ox, though vast in bulk, is kept on the road by a little whip.

Sophocles

THERE is no real elevation of mind in a contempt of little things. It is, on the contrary, from too narrow views that we consider those things of little importance, which have, in fact, such extensive consequences.

François de Fénelon

WITHOUT mounting by degrees, a man cannot attain to high things; and the breaking of the ladder still casteth a man back, and maketh the thing wearisome, which was easy.

Sir Philip Sidney

A STRAY hair, by its continued irritation, may give more annoyance than a smart blow.

James Russell Lowell

FLOWER in the crannied wall,
I pluck you out of the crannies,
I hold you here, root and all, in my hand,
Little flower — but if I could understand
What you are, root and all, and all in all,
I should know what God and man is.

Alfred, Lord Tennyson

LITTLE said is soonest mended.

George Wither

IF the nose of Cleopatra had been a little shorter, it would have changed the history of the world.

Blaise Pascal

IF God gives us but little tasks, let us be content to do little. It is pride and self-will which says: "Give me something great to do; I should enjoy that; but why make me sweep the dust?"

Charles Kingsley

THE smallest effort is not lost,
Each wavelet on the ocean tost
Aids in the ebb-tide or the flow;
Each rain-drop makes some floweret blow;
Each struggle lessens human woe.

Charles Mackay

WE are such little men when the stars come out.

Herman Hagedorn

HE that high growth on cedars did bestow,
Gave also lowly mushrumps leave to grow.

Robert Southwell

HOSPITALITY consists in a little fire, a little food, and an immense quiet.

Ralph Waldo Emerson

THE great moments of life are but moments like the others. Your doom is spoken in a word or two. A single look from the eyes, a mere pressure of the hand, may decide it, or of the lips, though they cannot speak.

William Makepeace Thackeray

MORE than one cigar at a time is excessive smoking.

Mark Twain

THINK naught a trifle, though it small appear;
Small sands the mountain, moments make the
    year,
And trifles life.

Edward Young

GOOD things, when short, are twice as good.

Baltasar Gracián

WHOEVER gives a small coin to a poor man has six blessings bestowed upon him, but he who speaks a kind word to him obtains eleven blessings.

Talmud

IT is the fixed law of the universe, that little things are but parts of the great. The grass does not spring up full grown, by eruptions: it rises by an increase so noiseless and gentle, as not to disturb an angel's ear — perhaps to be invisible to an angel's eye. The rain does not fall in masses, but in drops, or even in the breath-like moisture of the fine mist. The planets do not leap from end to end of their orbits, but inch by inch, and line by line, it is that they circle the heavens. Intellect, feeling, habit, character, all become what they are through the influence of little things. And in morals and religion, it is by little things — by little influences acting on us, or seemingly little decisions made by us, that everyone of us is going, not by leaps, yet surely by inches, either to life or death eternal.

Tryon Edwards

HE that steals an egg will steal an ox.

George Herbert

FROM a little spark may burst a mighty flame.

Dante

THE tree which needs two arms to span its girth sprang from the tiniest shoot. Yon tower, nine stories high, rose from a little mound of earth. A journey of a thousand miles began with a single step.

Lao-tsze

USE well the moment; what the hour
Brings for thy use is in thy power;
And what thou best canst understand
Is just the thing lies nearest to thy hand.

Johann Wolfgang von Goethe

REMEMBER this, — that very little is needed to make a happy life.

Marcus Aurelius

ALL the darkness of the world cannot put out the light of one small candle.

Anonymous

A MAN is in general better pleased when he has a good dinner upon his table, than when his wife talks Greek.

Samuel Johnson

MANY men fail in life, from the want, as they are too ready to suppose, of those great occasions wherein they might have shown their trustworthiness and integrity. But all such persons should remember, that in order to try whether a vessel be leaky, we first prove it with water, before we trust it with wine. The more minute and trivial opportunities of being just and upright, are constantly occurring to everyone; and it is an unimpeachable character in these lesser things that prepares and produces those very opportunities of greater advancement, and of higher confidence, which turn out so rich a harvest, but which only those are permitted to reap who have previously sown.

Charles Caleb Colton

Go not abroad for happiness. For see,
It is a flower that blossoms at thy door.

Minot J. Savage

THREE things are good in little measure and evil in large: yeast, salt, and hesitation.

Talmud

THE influences of little things are as real, and as constantly about us, as the air we breathe or the light by which we see. These are the small — the often invisible — the almost unthought of strands, which are inweaving and twisting by millions, to bind us to character — to good or evil here, and to heaven or hell hereafter.

Tryon Edwards

THE mouse that hath but one hole is quickly taken.

George Herbert

NOTHING can be done except little by little.

Charles Baudelaire

A MAN who cannot tolerate small ills can never accomplish great things.

Chinese Proverb

ONE half the troubles of this life can be traced to saying yes too quick, and not saying no soon enough.

Josh Billings

ANIMAL and vegetable organisms do not change by large and few convulsions but by small ones and many of them. So for the most part do states and men's opinions.

Samuel Butler

WE blame others for slight things, and over-look greater in ourselves.

Thomas à Kempis

HE that despiseth small things, shall fall by little by little.

Ecclesiasticus

ALAS, how easily things go wrong!
A sigh too much, or a kiss too long,
And there follows a mist and a weeping rain,
And life is never the same again.

George Macdonald

GOD requires a faithful fulfillment of the merest trifle given us to do, rather than the most ardent aspiration to things to which we are not called.

St. Francis de Sales

HAVE you ever had your day suddenly turn sunshiny because of a cheerful word? Have you ever wondered if this could be the same world, because someone had been unexpectedly kind to you? You can make today the same for somebody. It is only a question of a little imagination, a little time and trouble. Think now, "What can I do today to make someone happy?" — old persons, children, servants — even a bone for the dog, or sugar for the bird!

Maltbie Davenport Babcock

THE dangerous bar in the harbor's mouth is only grains of sand.

Martin Farquhar Tupper

IF we take a farthing from a thousand pounds, it will be a thousand pounds no longer.

Oliver Goldsmith

THESE are small things, but it was not by despising those small things that our ancestors accomplished this very great thing.

Titus Livius Livy

LIKE flakes of snow that fall imperceptibly upon the earth, the seemingly unimportant events of life succeed one another. As the snowflakes gather, so our *habits* are formed. No single flake that is added to the pile produces a sensible change. No single action creates, however it may exhibit, a man's character. But as the tempest hurls the avalanche down the mountain and overwhelms the inhabitant and his habitation, so *passion*, acting on the elements of mischief which pernicious habits have brought together, may overthrow the edifice of truth and virtue.

Jeremy Bentham

A WORD spoken in due season, how good it is!

Proverbs 15:23

THE shell must break before the bird can fly.

Alfred, Lord Tennyson

FOR the maintenance of peace, nations should avoid the pin-pricks which forerun cannon-shots.

Napoleon

By going a few minutes sooner or later, by stopping to speak with a friend on the corner, by meeting this man or that, or by turning down this street instead of the other, we may let slip some impending evil, by which the whole current of our lives would have been changed.

Henry Wadsworth Longfellow

Since trifles make the sum of human things,
And half our misery from our foibles springs;
Since life's best joys consist in peace and ease;
And though but few can serve yet all may
    please;
O! let th' ungentle spirit learn from hence,
A small unkindness is a great offence.
To spread large bounties though we wish in
    vain
Yet all may shun the guilt of giving pain.

Hannah More

All difficult things have their origin in that which is easy, and great things in that which is small.

Lao-tsze

NOTHING is small or great in God's sight. Whatever He wills becomes great to us, however seemingly trifling; and if once the voice of conscience tells us that He requires anything of us, we have no right to measure its importance.

Jean Nicholas Grau

No rock so hard but that a little wave
May beat admission in a thousand years.

Alfred, Lord Tennyson

LEARN to live, and live to learn,
Ignorance like a fire doth burn,
Little tasks make large return.

Bayard Taylor

HE who can take no interest in what is small will take false interest in what is great.

John Ruskin

THERE are single thoughts that contain the essence of a whole volume, single sentences that have the beauties of a large work.

Joseph Joubert

RESOLVE to do a little reading every day, if it is but a single sentence. If you gain fifteen minutes a day, it will make itself felt at the end of the year.

Horace Mann

FOR the want of a nail the shoe was lost,
For the want of a shoe the horse was lost,
For the want of a horse the rider was lost,
For the want of a rider the battle was lost,
For the want of a battle the kingdom was
    lost —
And all for want of a horseshoe-nail.

Benjamin Franklin

TIME is so precious that it is dealt out to us only in the smallest possible fractions — a tiny moment at a time.

Irish Proverb

A LITTLE and a little, collected together, become a great deal; the heap in the barn consists of single grains, and drop and drop make the inundation.

Saadi

THE manner in which one single ray of light, one single precious hint, will clarify and energize the whole mental life of him who receives it, is among the most wonderful and heavenly of intellectual phenomena.

Arnold Bennett

SHE doeth little kindnesses
Which most leave undone, or despise.

James Russell Lowell

FEW are so small or weak, I guess,
But may assist us in distress,
Nor shall we ever, if we're wise,
The meanest, or the least, despise.

[The Lion and the Mouse]

Jeffreys Taylor

A LITTLE fact is worth a whole limbo of dreams.

Ralph Waldo Emerson

JUNE reared that bunch of flowers you carry,
From seeds of April's sowing.

Robert Browning

IT is not of so much consequence what you say, as how you say it. Memorable sentences are memorable on account of some single ir-radiating word.

Alexander Smith

'Tis a little thing
To give a cup of water; yet its draught
Of cool refreshment, drained by fevered lips,
May give a shock of pleasure to the frame
More exquisite than when nectarean juice
Renews the life of joy in happier hours.
It is a little thing to speak a phrase
Of common comfort which by daily use
Has almost lost its sense, yet on the ear
Of him who thought to die unmourned 'twill
    fall
Like choicest music, fill the glazing eye
With gentle tears, relax the knotted hand
To know the bonds of fellowship again;
And shed on the departing soul a sense,
More precious than the benison of friends
About the honored deathbed of the rich,
To him who else were lonely, that another
Of the great family is near and feels.

Sir Thomas N. Talfourd

WHATEVER a man's age, he can reduce it several years by putting a bright-colored flower in his buttonhole.

Mark Twain

TROUBLES are like babies — they only grow by nursing.

Douglas Jerrold

My mind lets go a thousand things,
Like dates of wars and deaths of kings,
And yet recalls the very hour —
'Twas noon by yonder village tower,
And on the last blue noon in May
The wind came briskly up this way,
Crisping the brook beside the road;
Then, pausing here, set down its load
Of pine scents, and shook listlessly
Two petals from that wild-rose tree.

Thomas Bailey Aldrich

THE mighty are brought low by many a thing
Too small to name. Beneath the daisy's disk
Lies hid the pebble for the fatal sling.

Helen Hunt Jackson

49

I WOULD say to every person read with your pencil. Never pass a word, or an allusion, or a name you do not understand without marking it down for inquiry. Then go to your dictionary for the definition or explanation; go to the encyclopedia for information as to biographical or historical allusions. Never read about any country without having a map before you. This kind of study will fix things in your minds as no formal method of the school ever will.

Henry Ward Beecher

THE drying up a single tear has more
Of honest fame than shedding seas of gore.

Lord Byron

IF I can not do great things, I can do small things in a great way.

James Freeman Clarke

THERE is no beautifier of complexion, or form, or behavior, like the wish to scatter joy and not pain around us.

Ralph Waldo Emerson

MAKE a rule, and pray God to help you to keep it, never, if possible, to lie down at night without being able to say, "I have made one human being, at least, a little wiser, a little happier, or a little better this day."

Charles Kingsley

A LITTLE learning is a dangerous thing;
Drink deep, or taste not the Pierian spring:
There shallow draughts intoxicate the brain,
And drinking largely sobers us again.

Alexander Pope

THE smallest candle fills a mile with its rays, and the papillae of a man runs out to every star.

Ralph Waldo Emerson

BETTER one bite of the peach of immortality than a whole basket of apricots.

Chinese Proverb

THE glow of one warm thought is to me worth more than money.

Thomas Jefferson

IT is in those acts which we call trivialities
that the seeds of joy are forever wasted.

George Eliot

IT may be glorious to write
 Thoughts that will glad the two or three
High souls, like those far stars that come in
  sight
 Once in a century; —
But better far it is to speak
 One simple word, which now and then
Shall waken their free natures in the weak
 and friendless sons of men.

James Russell Lowell

THE little sweet doth kill much bitterness.

John Keats

AFFECTION, like melancholy, magnifies trifles.

Leigh Hunt

IF I can put one touch of rosy sunset into the
life of any man or woman, I shall feel that I
have worked with God.

George Macdonald

WE are spinning our own fates, good or evil, never to be undone. Every smallest stroke of virtue or vice leaves its ever-so-little scar. The drunken Rip Van Winkle, in Jefferson's play, excuses himself for every fresh dereliction by saying, "I won't count this time!" Well, he may not count it, and a kind Heaven may not count it; but it is being counted none the less. Down among his nerve-cells and fibers the molecules are counting it, registering and storing it up to be used against him when the next temptation comes. Nothing we ever do is, in strict scientific literalness, wiped out.

William James

ALL common things — each day's events,
    That with the hour begin and end;
Our pleasures and our discontents,
    Are rounds by which we may ascend.

Henry Wadsworth Longfellow

A STALE article, if you dip it in a good, warm, sunny smile, will go off better than a fresh one that you've scowled upon.

Nathaniel Hawthorne

EVEN the tiny, hard-working ant drags all she can with her mouth, and adds it to the heap she is building, because she is not heedless of the morrow.

Horace

"A COMMONPLACE life," we say, and we sigh,
But why should we sigh as we say?
The commonplace sun in the commonplace
   sky
Makes up the commonplace day;
The moon and the stars are commonplace
   things,
And the flower that blooms, and the bird
   that sings,
But dark were the world, and sad our lot,
If the flowers failed, and the sun shone not;
And God, who studies each separate soul,
Out of commonplace lives makes His
   beautiful whole.

Susan Coolidge

READ the best books first, or you may not have a chance to read them at all.

Henry David Thoreau

55

THE sound of a kiss is not so loud as that of a cannon, but its echo lasts a great deal longer.

Oliver Wendell Holmes

YOU mayn't be changed to a bird though you
    live
  As selfishly as you can;
But you will be changed to a smaller thing —
  A mean and selfish man.

Phoebe Cary

EXACTNESS in little things is a wonderful source of cheerfulness.

Frederick William Faber

IN life's small things be resolute and great
To keep thy muscle trained: know'st thou
    when Fate
Thy measure takes, or when she'll say to thee,
"I find thee worthy; do this deed for me?"

James Russell Lowell

A PRAYER in its simplest definition is merely a wish turned God-ward.

Phillips Brooks

EVERY man feels instinctively that all the beautiful sentiments in the world weigh less than a single lovely action.

James Russell Lowell

IT's just the little homely things,
The unobtrusive friendly things,
The "won't-you-let-me-help-you" things
    That make our pathway light.

Grace Haines

ONE dark cloud can hide the sunlight;
Loose one string, the pearls are scattered;
Think one thought, a soul may perish;
Say one word, a heart may break.

Adelaide Ann Proctor

A SLIP of the Foot you may soon recover,
But a slip of the Tongue you may never get
    over.

Benjamin Franklin

WHAT we call the little things are merely the causes of great things.

Henri Fréderic Amiel

58

TAKE care of the pence, and the pounds will take care of themselves.

Benjamin Franklin

AN ounce of work is worth many pounds of words.

St. Francis de Sales

IN every seed to breathe the flower,
In every drop of dew
To reverence a cloistered star
Within the distant blue;
To wait the promise of the bow
Despite the cloud between,
Is Faith — the fervid evidence
Of loveliness unseen.

John Banister Tabb

A MULTITUDE of small delights constitutes happiness.

Charles Baudelaire

Do not accustom yourself to use big words for little matters.

Samuel Johnson

PITHY sentences are like sharp nails which force truth upon our memory.

Denis Diderot

ALL of nature is to be found in the smallest things.

Latin Proverb

'TIS not in the high stars alone,
Nor in the cups of budding flowers,
Nor in the redbreast's mellow tone,
Nor in the bow that smiles in showers,
But in the mud and scum of things
There alway, alway something sings.

Ralph Waldo Emerson

To see the world in a grain of sand,
    And a heaven in a wild flower;
Hold infinity in the palm of your hand,
    And eternity in an hour.

William Blake

WE confess our little faults only to persuade others that we have no great ones.

François, Duc de la Rochefoucauld

WRINKLES should merely indicate where smiles have been.

Mark Twain

A LITTLE sun, a little rain,
    O soft wind blowing from the West,
And woods and fields are sweet again
    And Warmth within the mountain's breast.

A little love, a little trust,
    A soft impulse, a sudden dream,
And life as dry as desert dust,
    Is fresher than a mountain stream.

Stopford A. Brooke

OH, what a little thing can turn
A heavy heart from sighs to song!
A smile can make the world less stern,
A word can cause the soul to burn
With glow of heaven, all night long.

Anonymous

REMEMBER very slight things make epochs in married life.

George Eliot

You can count the apples on a tree, but you cannot count the trees in an apple.

African Proverb

Touch us gently, Time!
  We've not proud nor soaring wings:
Our ambition, our content,
  Lies in simple things.

Bryan Waller Proctor

Do the work that's nearest,
  Though it's dull at whiles,
Helping, when you meet them,
  Lame dogs over stiles;
See in every hedgerow
  Marks of angels' feet
Epics in each pebble
  Underneath our feet.

Charles Kingsley

In a child's lunch basket, a mother's thoughts.

Japanese Proverb